STAGE BY STAGE

Student's Book

John Dougill and Liz Doherty

HODDER AND STOUGHTON
LONDON SYDNEY AUCKLAND TORONTO

Acknowledgements

The publishers would like to thank Cadbury–Schweppes for permission to reproduce the photograph on page 40.

Illustrations by Linda Rogers Associates (Maggie Ling) and Tony Mould.

British Library Cataloguing in Publication Data
Dougill, John
    Stage by stage.
    Student's book
    1. English language – Text-books for
    foreign students
    I. Title   II. Doherty, Liz
    428.2'4   PE1128
    ISBN 0 340 37224 9

Typeset in 10/11pt Univers Medium by
Rowland Phototypesetting Ltd, Bury St Edmunds, Suffolk.

Printed and bound in Great Britain for Hodder and Stoughton Educational, a division of Hodder and Stoughton Ltd, Mill Road, Dunton Green, Sevenoaks, Kent by Anchor Brendon Limited, Tiptree, Essex

Contents

Unit 1   What do you think of the party?   4

Unit 2   This is a hold-up   11

Unit 3   Tall, dark and handsome   18

Unit 4   Have you got anything to declare?   24

Unit 5   What seems to be the trouble?   30

Unit 6   Could you tell me . . .?   36

Unit 7   Could I see the menu?   42

Unit 8   Do-It-Yourself   48

Unit 9   Can I help you?   53

Unit 10 Why don't you try the South of France?   59

UNIT 1

What do you think of the party?

Introduction

1 Introductions *These phrases will be useful in Stage 1.*
Match the sentences in column A with those in B.

A	B
I'm sure I've seen you before.	No. My name's Mary Shields.
How do you do?	Carolyn. What's yours?
My name's Peter. Peter Brown.	Yes, you look familiar too.
I don't think we've met, have we?	How do you do?
Sorry, what did you say your name was?	Pleased to meet you.

4

2 Describing character-type

This vocabulary will be useful in Stage 1.
Look at the following adjectives and see if you can match them to the definitions below.

Shy   Talkative   Thoughtful   Amusing   Lively   Snobbish   RUDE   Reserved   Miserable   Friendly

ⓐ Someone who likes chatting.
ⓑ A person who lacks confidence when meeting others.
ⓒ Someone who doesn't show her feelings very easily.
ⓓ This person makes you smile or laugh.
ⓔ There's never a dull moment with this person, as she's bright and cheerful.
ⓕ It's not much fun talking to this person.
ⓖ Someone who seems to be thinking of other things.
ⓗ This person might say something unpleasant to you.
ⓘ Someone who looks down on others and considers himself superior.
ⓙ This person is always kind and glad to meet others.

3 Open-ended dialogue

This dialogue will be necessary in Stage 1.
Look at the following dialogue. How do you imagine that it might continue? Write 5 to 10 lines and try to complete it.

A I hate parties, don't you?
B Well, it depends on the party. Sometimes they're quite fun.
A I don't know. I always promise myself never to come to another one.
B Why did you come to this one, then?
A Because . . .

4 Socialising *This vocabulary will be especially useful in Stages 3 and 4.*

Bill meets Jane at a party. She's an old friend he hasn't seen for some time. Look at the dialogue below and try to put it in the right order. (The first one has been done for you.)

Bill What about you? Have you finished your studies yet? _____

Jane By the way, have you heard about Mary? _____

Bill Well, Good luck! _____

Jane Fine. How about you? _____

Bill Jane! Haven't seen you for ages! How are you? ___1___

Jane Oh, congratulations! _____

Bill Great! Sorry, I must just go and speak to Sarah over there. _____

Jane She's got a job as a stewardess with British Airways. _____

Bill No, what's happened to her? _____

Jane No, I've got my exams next week. _____

Bill Pretty good. I've just been promoted at work. _____

Stage 1

1 Circulating You will be given a character-type by the teacher. Walk around the room in any direction. When the teacher claps or shouts, introduce yourself to the nearest person in the manner indicated by your character-type. Afterwards, continue walking round the room until the next time the teacher tells you to introduce yourself. When you introduce yourself, pretend that the other person is a stranger and that you have never met him before. If you like, choose a different name for yourself. After the exercise try to guess the character-types of the other students.

2 Role play You are going to play a short scene from a party. The teacher will tell you the details about your role. During the exercise try to talk and behave as your role suggests.

3 Open-ended dialogue For this exercise you need to memorize the dialogue in part 3 of the Introduction. You also need to decide the mood or character of the two people involved. Work in pairs and continue the dialogue for as long as possible until you reach some sort of conclusion. Remember to act according to the character-type you have decided upon.

Stage 2

There is a party in progress and one person A is standing by the drinks table and serving drinks. B approaches and A offers her a drink.

      B I thought you might be here.
      A Ah, hello. How are you?
      B Not bad. What about you?
      A All right, I suppose.
5   B What are you drinking?
      A Some sort of wine. Do you want some?
      B No, I think I'd prefer beer. Have they got any?
      A Yes, there's some over there.
      (*B pours out a drink.*)
      B Well, what do you think of the party?
10   A It's not bad. I'm not really in the mood for a party,
          though.
      B Why's that?
      A I don't know, really. I suppose I'm a bit tired.
      (*During the last exchange C has approached the*
      table to get a drink. A offers C a drink but accidentally
      drops it.)
      A Oh, sorry about that.
15   C (*annoyed*) I should think so!
      A Don't worry. It's not too bad.
      C What do you mean? It's gone all over my trousers
          – I only bought them last week.
      A There's no need to shout.
20   C (*loudly*) I'm not shouting.
      A Yes, you are.
      C (*very loudly*) No, I'm not!
      B (*wanting to calm the situation*) Look, why don't
          you dry them with this?
25   C (*ignores B*) You should watch what you're doing!
      A What do you mean? It was your fault!
      B How about another drink? (*C ignores B*)
      C Anyway, don't I know you?
      B Do you want another drink? (*A ignores B*)
30   A You might do.
      C You didn't go to St Mark's School, did you?
      A Yes, I did actually.

1 Read the letter and decide who was at the party and what happened.

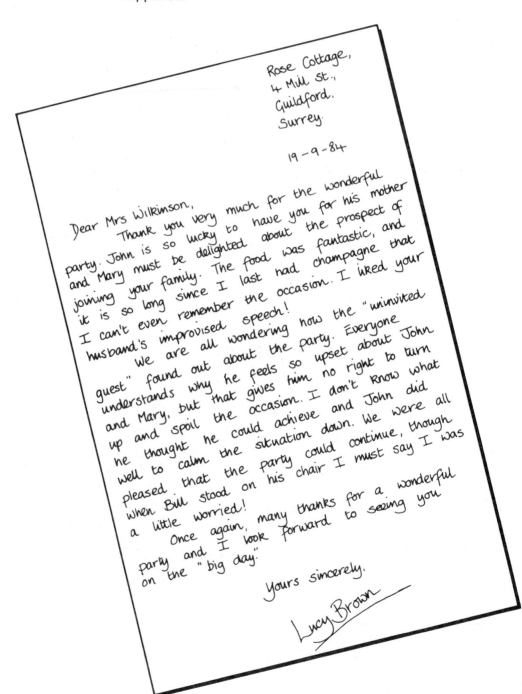

Rose Cottage,
4 Mill St.,
Guildford,
Surrey.

19 – 9 – 84

Dear Mrs Wilkinson,

Thank you very much for the wonderful party. John is so lucky to have you for his mother and Mary must be delighted about the prospect of joining your family. The food was fantastic, and it is so long since I last had champagne that I can't even remember the occasion. I liked your husband's improvised speech!

We are all wondering how the "uninvited guest" found out about the party. Everyone understands why he feels so upset about John and Mary, but that gives him no right to turn up and spoil the occasion. I don't know what he thought he could achieve and John did well to calm the situation down. We were all pleased that the party could continue, though when Bill stood on his chair I must say I was a little worried!

Once again, many thanks for a wonderful party and I look forward to seeing you on the "big day".

Yours sincerely,

Lucy Brown

Work in groups and decide the following points:
- what sort of party was it?
- was the food served at a table or at a buffet?
- what might the husband have spoken about?
- who was the uninvited guest and what did he come to do or say?
- why did Bill stand on his chair?

When you have sorted out these points, you can begin to work out how to act out the party scene.

2 Here are some lines taken from a party. Make up a sketch to include all the lines. It does not matter in what order they appear.

3 Look at the suggestions below and try to work out a sketch about a surprise party. Don't feel limited to the ideas provided – there are many other possibilities!

Several people are planning a surprise party.
Who is it for and why?   Someone's birthday.
                           Someone returning from abroad.
                           Someone's passed their exams.
                           Someone returning from hospital.

They succeed in surprising the person concerned.
How?   They turn up unexpectedly.
         They are waiting when the person returns.
         They wait in the dark.
         They hide behind the furniture.
         They take the person to an unexpected place.

The person concerned reacts according to his character/mood.
How do they react?   They're excited.
                       They're embarrassed.
                       They become angry.
                       They're suspicious.

However, something goes wrong.
What could it be?   They have got the wrong day.
                     They're in the wrong house.
                     The person has just had bad news.
                     Something gets broken.
                     The neighbours complain.

The evening continues but not as planned.
How?   They all go for a meal.
        They watch TV.
        They celebrate something else.
        They plan another surprise party.

UNIT 2

This is a hold-up

Introduction

1 Crimes *This vocabulary will be especially useful in Stages 1 and 3.*

FRAUD ARSON SHOPLIFTING MUGGING MURDER SMUGGLING BRIBERY ASSAULT VANDALISM FORGERY BURGLARY PICKING POCKETS

Choose one of these crimes to fit the following situations.

(a) Someone takes a pair of jeans from a clothes shop without paying for them.

(b) In a crowded bus a man takes a purse out of a woman's handbag.

(c) An old woman is walking down the street when suddenly someone runs up behind her, knocks her over and runs away with her handbag.

(d) A woman goes through Customs without saying anything about the ten bottles of duty-free whisky she has in her case.

(e) A drunk gets angry with someone and punches him in the face.

(f) A couple go out for the evening. When they return, they find that their house has been broken into and their valuables taken.

(g) In order to win business for his company, a manager pays a politician a lot of money.

(h) An old man is found stabbed to death by the side of the road.

(i) Some drunken youths break a shop window.

(j) Two people print their own banknotes and then go out shopping and buy everything they have ever wanted.

(k) A schoolboy hates his school so much that he sets fire to it and burns it down.

(l) A man knocks on people's doors and says he is collecting money for charity. In fact he is a thief.

2 Criminal phrases   *This vocabulary will be useful in Stages 1 and 3.*

Match the phrases in column A with the list of criminals in B.

A	B
(a) If you want to see your wife again, bring the money to the station tonight.	i) a hijacker
(b) Take this plane to Cuba.	ii) a drug dealer
(c) Hand over the money or I'll shoot.	iii) a kidnapper
(d) Unless you give me the money tomorrow I'm going to tell the newspapers.	iv) a terrorist
	v) a bankrobber
(e) The bomb will go off at exactly 5.30.	vi) a blackmailer
(f) It's £20.00 a gramme.	

3 Bank transactions   The sketch in Stage 2 takes place in a bank. It will help if you are familiar with some of the language used in banks.
The following dialogue between a bank clerk and a customer is in the wrong order. Show the right order by numbering each sentence. (The first and the last ones have been done for you.)

Clerk   Right, that's fine. Anything else?   _____

Customer   Can I have five ones and the rest in fives, please?   _____

Clerk   Could you sign it on the back?   _____

Customer   Yes, I'd like to cash this cheque.   _____

Clerk   Could you tell me your account number, please?   _____

Customer   Oh, sorry. I forgot to fill it in. It's 91150723.   _____

Clerk   Yes. Now, how would you like the money?   _____

Customer   Hello. I'd like to pay this into my account.   __1__

Clerk   Here you are. That's five ones and nine fives.   __10__

Customer   Where? Here?   _____

1 Chief Inspector Brown is in charge of a murder investigation. He has just visited the room where a body was found. Here is his report.

Statement by Chief Inspector Brown

At 19.00 hours on Friday 16th October the manager of the Queens Hotel telephoned the Police Station to report a suspected murder. A chambermaid had discovered a dead body in the hotel's luxury suite.

I went immediately to the hotel where I found the dead man lying face upwards in the middle of the room. He had obviously died from bullet wounds, one received in his arm and the other in his head. There were clear signs that a fight had taken place; most of the furniture had been smashed or turned upside-down. There was a gun in the dead man's hand and two shots had been fired from it. I could not find the discharged bullets in the room. I found a second gun by the door from which two shots had also been fired. Our forensic scientists have confirmed that the two bullets found in the dead man's body had been fired from this gun. A substantial amount of blood had soaked into the carpet. Some of this belonged to the dead man and some belonged to another person. In one corner of the room I found a suitcase containing three sawn-off shot guns, a make-up box, several masks and a number of wigs. Near to the up-turned table there were half a dozen empty champagne bottles, a number of broken glasses and a plan of Merchant's Bank (the bank which was robbed of £50,000 at 10.00 hours on Friday 16th October). Finally, I noted that about twenty new bank notes had been torn into pieces and thrown about the room.

I have nothing further to record at this point in the investigation.

- Can you work out what happened in the hotel room before the man's death?
- How do you explain the plan of the bank, the disguises and the shotguns?
- Why should there be champagne bottles?
- What was being celebrated and did someone get drunk?
- Why should the bank notes have been torn up?

● Why was there a fight and who did the dead man shoot?
Once you have decided what could have taken place in the room (there may be several interpretations) decide precisely how many people were involved. What kind of people were they? How did their moods change during their time in the room?
Now devise a scene to reconstruct exactly what took place in the room. Make sure you include **every** point made by Chief Inspector Brown.

2 At 14.00 hours on Monday, 14th January the passengers board British Airways flight 4352 from Heathrow Airport.
● What is the plane's destination?
● Who are the passengers and why are they travelling?
The passengers find their seats.
● How do they pass the time until take-off?
The steward/ess goes through the usual safety procedure and the captain makes an announcement. Soon after take-off someone tries to hijack the plane.
● Who is/are the hijacker/s?
● What do they threaten to do?
● Where do they want the plane to go? Why?
● How do the passengers and crew react?
Are the hijackers successful? If so, what happens to the passengers and how does the scene end? If not, what happens? Do the hijackers lose their nerve or are they overcome by the passengers and crew? What happens to the hijackers and how does the scene end?

3   A crime goes wrong.
What kind of crime could it be?

Robbery
Murder
A kidnapping
Blackmail
Fraud

What are the criminals like?

Professional or
inexperienced?
Intelligent or stupid?
Rich or poor?

What exactly do they plan to do?

What kind of victims do they encounter?

Surprised
Frightened
Brave
Aggressive

The criminals don't succeed.
Why not?   The criminals panic.
The victims fight back.
A policeman arrives.
The criminals don't understand each other.

UNIT 3

Tall, dark and handsome

Introduction

1 Parts of the body *This vocabulary will be useful in the exercises in Stage 1.*
Fill in the parts of the body indicated from the words in the box.

wrist	bottom	toes
thigh	heel	elbow
ankle	shoulder	back
knee	chest	waist
chin		

2 Instructions *The language involved in this exercise will be of use in Stage 1.*
Match the descriptions with the pictures.

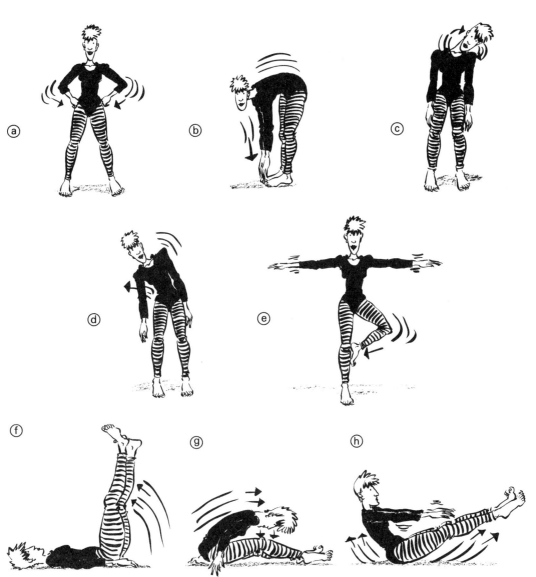

i) Bend forward and touch your toes.
ii) Stand with your legs apart and hands on your hips.
iii) Lie on your back with your legs pointing upwards.
iv) Stand on your right leg and put your left foot against your right knee.
v) Roll your head around in a circle.
vi) Lie down on the floor. Keeping your legs straight, bend forward until your head touches your knees.
vii) Bend sideways from the waist.
viii) Balance on your bottom holding your heels in the air.

3 Descriptions *This vocabulary will be needed in exercise 3 of Stage 1 and later on in the unit.*

There are mistakes in the following lists. Rearrange them so they are correct.

General	Age	Build	Hair	Height	Special Features
pretty	young	thin	a scar	short	a moustache
good-looking	bearded	slim	straight	medium-height	freckles
curly	middle-aged	medium-build	dyed	tall	spotty
hand-some	elderly	a good figure	balding	fat	wavy
plain	a teenager	plump	shoulder-length		false teeth
a double chin	in his/her thirties	ugly	bald		a wig

Stage 1

1 Simon says The teacher gives instructions but you should only carry out those instructions which begin with the words *Simon says*. In other words, you must obey Simon, not the teacher. Here is an example:

Teacher: *Simon says 'Touch your toes'.*	(You touch your toes.)
Teacher: *Simon says 'Touch your knees'.*	(You touch your knees.)
Teacher: *Now touch your elbows.*	(You don't do anything.)
Teacher: *Simon says 'Touch your elbows'.*	(You touch your elbows.)

2 Following instructions In this exercise you simply have to do what your teacher tells you. It will involve lying down on the floor, so make sure that you have enough space.

3 Mime Each student is given a description of a person by the teacher and then mimes what the description is. The rest of the class try to guess the **exact** words of the description – getting it nearly right isn't good enough!
Remember that the person miming should not speak.

Stage 2

A Scene at Perfect Partners Ltd, a dating agency where people hope to meet their partner for life.

A Good morning. Can I help you?

B Yes. I'd like to find my perfect partner.

A I see. Well, if you could just answer a few questions?

B Certainly.

5 A First of all, what age would you like your partner to be?

B About 20. Not more than 25, anyway.

A Okay. And what sort of build?

B What do you mean?

A Well, would you like someone who was very slim or would

10 you prefer someone rather more plump?

B Ah, I see. I don't think I mind, actually.

A And what about height?

B Oh, not too tall.

A So, medium-height?

15 B Yes, and long hair.

A Any particular colour?

B No. As long as it's long, it doesn't matter what colour.

A Good. Now, is there anything else at all?

B Well, obviously I'd like someone good-looking.

20 A Well, we'll see what we can do. Would you like to fill in this form in the next room and I'll call you soon.

(C enters)

C Hello. Is this the Perfect Partners office?

A That's right.

C I'm interested in meeting someone new.

25 A Well, you've certainly come to the right place. What sort of person are you looking for?

C Oh, someone tall, dark and handsome.

A I see. And what sort of age?

C Oh, mid-twenties, I suppose.

30 A Well, I might have just the person for you. Could I just ask how old you are?

C 24.

A Good. Could you just wait here a minute?

(C is puzzled.)

(A goes and fetches B.)

A This doesn't usually happen, but I think I've found just the

35 person for you.

B Oh, no!

C Not you!

B What are you doing here?

A I think I should be asking you that.

Stage 3

1 The scene is a police-station. There is a policeman or woman behind a desk.

What is he or she doing?   Tidying up.
Sorting through files.
Humming.
On the phone.

Two or three people enter very excitedly one after another.
What sort of people are they?   Shy.
Make sure each has a different character.   Loud.
Aggressive.
Foreign.
Old.
Arrogant.

They have all witnessed a crime being committed and have come to report it.
What kind of crime was it?   A burglary.
A robbery.
A car-theft.
A murder.
An assault.
A mugging.

They each try to describe the person who committed the crime, but each description is different.
How do they describe the criminal?   (*See Stage 1.*)
How does the policeman or woman react and what does he or she decide to do?   Gets angry and arrests all of them.
Sends them all away to argue with each other.
Asks them to take him or her to the scene of the crime.
Asks them to re-enact the crime.
Recognises one of them as the criminal and arrests him or her.

2 There is a beauty contest for Mr or Miss Universe. Each contestant has to parade on stage while the commentator describes him or her.

How will you parade?   All together in a circle
One by one to the front
Across the stage and turn round

Each contestant is then given a brief interview by the commentator.

What questions does he/she ask?   Their age
Their job
Their background
Their ambition

At the end the winner is announced either by the commentator or a judge. But then something unexpected happens.

What could it be?   The other competitors object.
The winner disagrees.
The commentator falls in love.
The winner is disqualified.

3

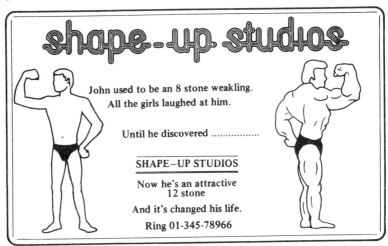

This advertisement appeared in the newspapers. Shape-Up now want to make a TV commercial about their studios. Your task is to produce the commercial.

You will probably want to show John's life as an 8 stone weakling and compare it with his life as a stronger, heavier man. You will want to show what happens at the studios. Perhaps you will claim that Shape-Up could improve the appearance of the TV viewers and invite them to the studios.

Decide how many people you will need for the commercial and what part each person will play. It might be a good idea for someone to introduce the commercial and explain what is going on. Perhaps you could make up a catchy song to go with it.

Make sure the commercial has a beginning, a middle and an end.

UNIT 4

Have you got anything to declare?

Introduction

1 Travel items *This vocabulary may be needed in exercise 1 of Stage 1 and in Stage 3.*
Match the following items with the list below.

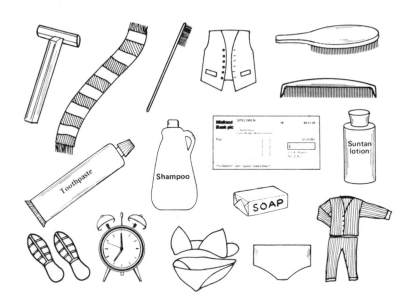

ⓐ an alarm-clock
ⓑ a comb
ⓒ a cheque-book
ⓓ sandals
ⓔ a bar of soap

ⓕ a razor
ⓖ a clothes-brush
ⓗ a waistcoat
ⓘ pyjamas
ⓙ swimming trunks

ⓚ a bikini
ⓛ suntan lotion
ⓜ a toothbrush
ⓝ shampoo
ⓞ toothpaste
ⓟ a scarf

2 Intentions

Asking and stating intentions will be part of exercise 3 in Stage 1 and might be useful in Stage 3.

Complete the following dialogue. Each gap represents one word.

A Hello Tim. Do you know where you're going for your holiday yet?

B Yes, I thought _____ try Spain.

A Really? Which part?

B Well, I was _____ _____ the north but I couldn't get a flight there, so I'm going to Madrid.

A How long have you got?

B A couple of weeks.

A You're _____ _____ in Madrid the whole time, are you?

B No, I'm thinking _____ _____ a car for a week.

A Are you going to do some touring?

B Yes, I'm not sure where, but I'm planning _____ _____ some of the towns in the south.

A Well, I can recommend Cordoba.

B Yes, that's one of the places _____ _____ intending _____ _____ .

A Okay, have a good time if I don't see you before you go.

3 At the customs

Apart from the situation in Stage 2, the language involved in Customs will be needed in Stage 3.

The following dialogue between a customs officer (C.O.) and a tourist (T.) is in the wrong order. Show the right order by numbering each sentence. (The first and last have been done for you.)

C.O. I see. And how long were you there for? _____

T. This one? But there are only old clothes in it. _____

C.O. Well, I'd like to have a look for myself, if you don't mind. _____

T. Spain and Morocco. _____

C.O. That's a long time. Did you buy any expensive items such as jewellery? _____

T. Just over two months. _____

C.O. Would you mind opening that case, please? _____

T. Oh, dear. __12__

C.O. Have you got anything to declare? _____

T. No, nothing expensive. Only this second-hand watch. _____

C.O. Hello. Could you tell me where you've been? __1__

T. Not really. Only the permitted amount of alcohol and tobacco. _____

Stage 1

1 Mime Mime taking an article out of a suitcase and doing something with it in order to show the rest of the class what it is. The teacher will tell you what to mime. Do not speak when you are miming but you can nod or shake your head.

2 Mirroring In pairs. One student mimes certain actions while the other tries to copy the movements as if reflecting them in a mirror. Your teacher will tell you what actions to mime. Make sure that movements are clear and slow.

3 Circulating Choose a holiday from a list provided by the teacher. Then move around the room and try to find others who have chosen the same holiday. When you find someone who has chosen exactly the same holiday as you, stay with him but continue trying to find others who have chosen the same. When you meet another student, your conversation might be something like this:

A Where are you planning to go?
B Greece. What about you?
A Greece too. Where are you going to stay?
B I'm camping.
A So am I. When are you going?
B In August.
A Oh, dear. I'm going in July.

4 Role-play In pairs. The two people involved are strangers, on a train heading for the south of France, who start talking to each other. Your teacher will give you instructions about the roles of the two people involved.

ASKED by the Belgian, customs if he had anything to declare, Mr Manju Turay of Gambia, said: "Yes, 55 lbs of cannabis," and was gaoled for three years.

Stage 2

The scene is at an airport. A man and a woman carrying several cases approach a customs officer.

    Him (*whispering*) Don't worry. Everything'll be all right.
    Her I hope you know what you're doing!
    (*They put their bags down in front of the customs officer.*)
    C.O. Good morning, sir, madam. Just returning from a
           holiday, are you?
5   *Her* That's right.
    C.O. And how long have you been abroad?
    Her Two weeks.
    Him Yes, not very long. Not long enough to buy anything
           anyway. (*laughs*)
10   *C.O.* I see. Have you got anything to declare?
    Him I'm sorry, I don't really know what you mean.
    Her Harry!
    C.O. Come on, sir. I'm sure you know what I mean. Have you
           got anything to declare?
15   *Him* Well . . . yes. I would like to declare that I love my wife.
    Her Oh, Harry. You've never said that before.
    Him Well, it's true! It's just that I've never been able to tell
           you before.
    Her And I love you too!
20   *C.O.* (*clears throat*) I'm sorry to interrupt, but I must ask you
           whether you have any goods to declare.
    Him Ah, well I do have a record-player, a fridge and
           something for my wife's birthday that I'd rather not tell
           you about.

25	*Her* Harry! And I thought you'd forgotten again!
	Him Of course not, dear!
	C.O. (*annoyed*) What I want to know, sir, is whether you have any goods in that bag that I should know about.
	Him Well, let's have a look. (*opens bag*) We've got some bars
30	of soap, a tube of toothpaste, clothes, a jar of cream . . .
	C.O. (*angry*) I only want to know if you have anything liable for tax, like cigarettes, perfumes or bottles of anything.
	Him Well, we do have a bottle of shampoo.
	C.O. Okay. I've had enough. You can go.
35	*Him* You mean that's it?
	C.O. Please go away!
	Her Come on, Harry. He just told us we could go.
	(*takes hold of the suitcase and the contents spill out*)

Stage 3

1 Read the following press report:

Top Musician in Drugs Shock

Thousands of fans had to wait several hours before their idol Johnnie Star emerged from customs at Gatwick Airport yesterday. Reporters and photographers had gathered with fans to see the long-awaited return of Johnnie to England after his successful world tour.

Johnnie refused to open his luggage on his way through customs and officials had to force open his bags against his wishes. Amongst his sequined suits and famous silver wigs, customs officials found £500 worth of marijuana. Multimillionaire Johnnie finally emerged from his ordeal. He is due to appear in court next week. Smiling and blowing kisses to his fans, he seemed undaunted by the experience. Johnnie said "The officials were a bit unfair. The drugs were for my own use. I can afford a £1,000 fine anytime." Customs officer Mike Jones said "We were only doing our job. It's difficult when you've got to search a famous guy like Johnnie Star. Actually he's one of my heroes."

Johnnie later returned to his country mansion where he is planning to throw a party to celebrate the end of his tour. As he left Gatwick he invited all his fans to his party to share his success. He even extended the invitation to Mike Jones.

Devise a scene around this report.
You will want to show what happened at Customs. How did the customs officer handle the situation? Johnnie said the officials were 'unfair', but at least one was a fan of his. How was the marijuana found? How did everyone react?
You will then want to show what happened when Johnnie emerged from Customs. How did he behave? How did the reporters and photographers react? What did the fans do? How does the scene end?

2 Make up a sketch to include all the following lines. It does not matter in what order they appear.

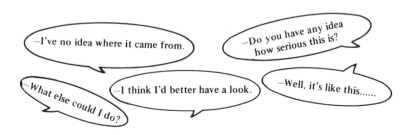

—I've no idea where it came from.

—Do you have any idea how serious this is?

—What else could I do?

—I think I'd better have a look.

—Well, it's like this......

3 A queue of people are waiting to go through Customs. One of them is smuggling something.

How do we know what kind of people they are?

By the way they stand
By the way they're dressed
By the type of baggage they carry
By what they say, if anything

The customs officer is thoroughly searching the baggage of the first person and asking questions about the contents.

How do the others react?

Impatient
Worried
Curious
Unconcerned

The smuggler decides to get rid of what he/she has by putting it in the bag of the next person to be searched. This person does not notice.

When he/she is searched, what happens?

The article is found.
The person is surprised.
The person sees the article first and hides it.
The person breaks down and cries.

What is the final outcome?

The person is arrested.
The smuggler tries to claim it back.
The customs officer realises what has happened.
The customs officer decides to keep the article.

UNIT 5

What seems to be the trouble?

Introduction

1 Complaints and illnesses *This vocabulary will be needed in the first exercise of Stage 1 and throughout the unit.*
For how many of the following would you *normally* go to the doctor? Count up how many and compare with others in the class.

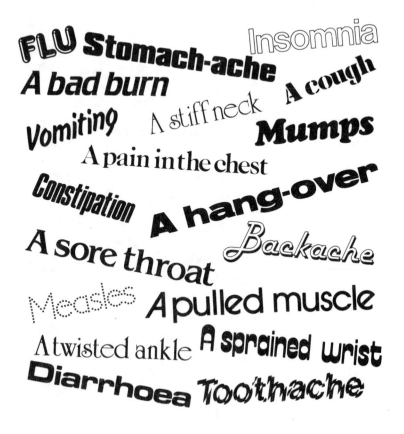

FLU Stomach-ache Insomnia
A bad burn A cough
Vomiting A stiff neck Mumps
A pain in the chest
Constipation A hang-over
A sore throat Backache
Measles A pulled muscle
A twisted ankle A sprained wrist
Diarrhoea Toothache

2 Giving advice *You will need to know how to give advice and make suggestions about remedies in exercise 2 in Stage 1 and later on in the unit.*

Match the sentences in Group A with those in Group B.

Group A	Group B
ⓐ Look at this bite – it's getting worse.	i) Have you tried holding your breath?
ⓑ Have you got any cough medicine?	ii) I've got some ointment upstairs. Why don't you try that?
ⓒ I just can't get rid of these hiccups.	iii) I don't know. Perhaps you should see a doctor.
ⓓ What do you think these bumps are?	iv) You ought to wear a bandage. That'll help support it.
ⓔ I've got a migraine coming on – give me another aspirin.	v) You shouldn't take so many.
ⓕ I can hardly walk: I think I've sprained my ankle.	vi) No, I haven't. I'd have some lemon and honey, if I were you.

3 Doctor and patient *The language in the dialogue below will be of use throughout the unit.*

The following dialogue is in the wrong order. Show the right order by numbering each sentence. (The first and last have been done for you.)

Doctor No, I'm sure it isn't, but I'm going to give you a prescription and I want you to take a couple of days off work. _____

Patient I think I've got some kind of fever. _____

Doctor Come in. What's the problem? __1__

Patient How long do you think it will last? _____

Doctor I see. What exactly's the matter? _____

Patient Well, I've been feeling a bit off colour for a few days and, you know, I've had a headache, sore throat and generally feel run down. _____

Doctor Not very long. Make another appointment with the receptionist for Tuesday. __9__

Patient Okay. I hope it's nothing serious. _____

Doctor Mm, I'd better take your pulse and temperature. _____

Stage 1

1 Mime Each student in turn mimes a particular illness. The rest of the class try to guess what it is. Your teacher will suggest to you what you should mime. Remember that you should not say anything when you are miming.

2 Giving advice Half the class are ill or unwell for one reason or another. The other half of the class move about the room giving them advice as to what they should do.

Example:
A Hello. What's the matter with you?
B I've got terrible toothache.
A I see. Have you seen a dentist?
B Yes, I've got an appointment tomorrow.
A Well, if I were you, I'd take a couple of aspirin.

or

C Hello. What's wrong with you?
D I've got an awful sore throat.
C Why don't you have a hot drink of something like tea and lemon?
D I've already tried that.
C Well, maybe you should put some whisky in it as well.
D That sounds a good idea. Thanks.

3 Matching lines Each student is given a line by the teacher to memorize. Each line has a matching line, for example:

You don't look very well.   ⓐ It's in the drawer.
            ⓑ Why don't you try sello-tape.
            ⓒ No, I've got a terrible headache.

The matching line is ⓒ. You have to find the person whose line matches yours. Afterwards, improvise a short scene that includes both lines.

Stage 2

The scene is a doctor's waiting room, where there are three chairs. Enter first patient holding stomach and groaning. She sits down with a pained expression.

Enter second patient with backache.
 Second patient 'Morning.
  First patient 'Morning.
 Second patient Have you been waiting long?
  First patient Not really, but it feels like hours.
5 *Second patient* Yes, I know what you mean.
(Enter a third patient with arm in a sling)
  Third patient 'Morning.
    First &
 Second patient 'Morning.
  Third patient Have you been waiting long?
 Second patient Not really. I've only just arrived.
10 *Third patient* Let's hope we don't have to wait too long.
(Enter a fourth patient with a limp)
 Fourth patient 'Morning.
    Others 'Morning.

	Fourth patient	Have you been waiting long?
	First patient	Quite long.
15	Second patient	About ten minutes (*at the same time*)
	Third patient	Not too long.

(Patient 4 looks around for somewhere to sit and sees there isn't anywhere. He obviously wants to sit. Patient 1 is holding her stomach.)

	Fourth patient	You've got a stomach-ache, have you?
	First patient	Yes. It must have been something I ate.
	Fourth patient	It could be food-poisoning. When I had that,
20		the doctor gave me some really horrible medicine which made me feel worse. I had to take a week off work.
	First patient	Really? (*looks worried*)
	Fourth patient	Yes. And then a friend told me to stop eating
25		for a day and just drink water.
	First patient	What happened? Did it work?
	Fourth patient	Of course. If I were you, I'd try it. Anything's better than that medicine.
	First patient	Mm. Yes, that sounds a good idea. I'll give it
30		a try. Thanks a lot. (*goes, still clutching stomach*)

(Patient 4 sits down and after a moment turns to patient 2.)

	Fourth patient	What's your problem?
	Second patient	I've got this terrible backache.
	Fourth patient	But there's nothing doctors can do about backache! They just give you painkillers.
35	Second patient	That might help!
	Fourth patient	True, but you really ought to try sleeping on a hard mattress. That would soon get rid of it.
	Second patient	Are you sure?
	Fourth patient	Yes. I used to have really bad backache until I
40		got a hard mattress. I never had any trouble after that.
	Second patient	Mm. I've heard that before. Perhaps that is the best thing. Thanks. (*goes*)

(Patient 4 moves along a seat and after a moment turns to patient 3.)

	Fourth patient	Nothing serious, I hope?
45	Third patient	It's pretty bad. I got bitten by a dog.

�▪ Stage 3

1 Some people are having a conversation at breakfast.
Who are they?   A family
                  Friends at a hotel
                  Students

What are they talking about?   What happened last night
                                 Another person
                                 What they will do that day

Someone enters who is not feeling well. He explains to the others what is wrong.

What is wrong with him?
A hang-over
Stomach-ache
A stiff back

The others try to give him advice but none of it is suitable.

What does he say?
I've tried that before.
I don't think that'll work.
I'm not very keen on . . .

A visitor arrives and suddenly all is well with the person. Why?

Who is the visitor?
A teacher
A girlfriend
The father/mother

2 Some friends want to go out and do something.

Where do they want to go?
The cinema
A pub
To visit someone
To play something

One of the friends is feeling unwell and doesn't want to go.

What's wrong with the person?
A headache
Depressed
Flu
A sore throat

The others make suggestions and try to persuade him/her to go with them.

What do they suggest?
Why don't you . . .
Have you tried . . .

The friend doesn't want to go with the others and the others leave.

How does the friend refuse?
I don't feel like . . . ing
I'm not in the mood for . . .
I'd like to, but . . .
It's just too painful.

Later on the friends return.

What do they find?
The friend is enjoying him/herself.
The friend has a special visitor.
The friend's condition has got worse.

3 A drug company has invented a new pill. They claim that it will cure *all* illnesses and they are marketing it under the name of SUPERPILL.

The company have decided to make a TV commercial to promote their product. Your task is to produce the commercial. How will you sell SUPERPILL? You could show people with various illnesses and their remarkable recovery after taking SUPERPILL. Perhaps you could explain how SUPERPILL was invented and say why it is better than all the other drugs on the market. Most successful commercials include a catchy tune or song. Make sure it has a beginning, middle and end.

UNIT 6

Could you tell me...?

Introduction

1 Jobs (1) *This vocabulary will be useful for the warm-up exercises of Stage 1 and for Stage 3.*
Match the following objects with the list of jobs below.

(a) a nurse
(b) a gardener
(c) a vet
(d) a musician

(e) a pilot
(f) a waiter
(g) a decorator
(h) a carpenter

(i) a librarian
(j) a postman
(k) a fisherman

2 Jobs (2)   *Here is some more vocabulary that will be of use for Stage 1 and Stage 3.*

Match the statements with the jobs.

(a) Someone who works out a company's financial situation.
(b) Someone who installs and repairs pipes and water-systems.
(c) Someone who prepares and sells meat.
(d) Someone who prepares legal documents such as wills.
(e) Someone who sells fruit and vegetables.
(f) Someone who works under-ground and digs for coal.
(g) Someone who designs houses.
(h) Someone who writes books.
(i) Someone who works for a government department.
(j) Someone who makes bread.
(k) Someone who deals with enquiries.
(l) Someone who takes pictures of people and events.

i) a lawyer
ii) a miner
iii) a baker
iv) an author
v) a civil servant
vi) a greengrocer
vii) a butcher
viii) a receptionist
ix) a plumber
x) an architect
xi) a photographer
xii) an accountant

3 Jobs (3)   *Here is further vocabulary that will be of use in Stage 1 and 3.*

In each of the following groups decide which one *usually* earns the most money.

(a) a farmworker – a secretary – a bank clerk – a dentist – a stewardess.
(b) a dustman – an engineer – a policeman – a lecturer – a surgeon.
(c) a bus-conductor – a factory-worker – a caretaker – a shop-assistant – a builder.
(d) a judge – a social worker – a teacher – a journalist – a hairdresser.
(e) an artist – a company director – an editor – a politician – a salesman.

4 Interviewing   *In this unit you will need to be able to ask polite, formal questions. This exercise is to give you practice in doing that.*

Mr Large is interviewing Miss Jones for the job of receptionist in his company. Complete the part of Mr Large.

Mr Large Come in, Miss Jones, and sit down.
Miss Jones Thank you.
Mr Large Would you mind telling me ....?
Miss Jones I'm unemployed.
Mr Large And have you ....?
Miss Jones Yes, I worked for a company for six months last year.
Mr Large Could you ....?
Miss Jones Yes, it was Freemason and Co.

Mr Large	I will of course require references. Would it be all right ....?
Miss Jones	Yes, certainly.
Mr Large	Now I wonder if you could tell me ....?
Miss Jones	Well, the reason I chose this particular job is because your company has such a good reputation.
Mr Large	I see. Are there any ....?
Miss Jones	No, I think your secretary told me everything I wanted to know.
Mr Large	Fine. There's just one more thing: when would you ....?
Miss Jones	I could start straightaway.
Mr Large	Right, Miss Jones. We'll be in touch as soon as we've reached a decision. Thank you very much for coming.

Stage 1

1 Guessing game One student thinks of a job and the others try to find out what it is by asking questions. The person answering may only say yes or no.

It is more useful to begin with general questions rather than asking 'Are you a butcher?' Here are some questions that might be useful:

- do you work indoors?
- do you wear special clothes?
- do you need training for the job?
- do you use special tools or instruments?
- do you earn a lot of money?
- is your job usually done by women?

2 Mime Each student thinks of a job (or is given one by the teacher) and has to show the rest of the class what it is by a short mime. When someone has guessed the job correctly, the next student takes a turn.

When you are miming, remember not to say anything.

3 Competitive mime In groups. One member of each group goes to the teacher, who whispers to him the first job on a list. The students mime to their group what the job is. As soon as someone guesses correctly, he goes to the teacher, who whispers to him the next job on the list. The winning group is the one that gets to the end of the list first.

4 Role play There is an interview for the job of sports teacher. Work in pairs with one student being the employer and the other playing the part of an applicant for the job. Your teacher will give you instructions about the details of the two roles.

Stage 2

A director is interviewing and auditioning three people for the part of Hamlet. The three applicants are sitting at the side. One is very quiet and nervous, one has difficulty remembering and the third has a cold.

	Director	Right! Could we have the first person please?
	Applicant 1	(*in a very quiet voice*) Jones.
	Director	Now, there's no need to be nervous. Could you tell me what jobs you've done before?
5	*Applicant 1*	Well, I used to work in a library. Before that I was a music teacher.
	Director	I see. And would you mind telling me why you want to act in this play?
	Applicant 1	I just wanted a change of job.
10	*Director*	Pardon?
	Applicant 1	I said I wanted a change of job.
	Director	Okay. Let's hear the speech then.
	Applicant 1	To be or not to be, that is the question! Whether . . .
15	*Director*	No, I'm sorry. It's just too quiet. I need someone with more confidence. Who's next?
	(*No. 3 nudges No. 2*)	
	Applicant 2	Ah, that's me.
	Director	Okay. What's your name?
	Applicant 2	Joe. Joe Bloggs.
20	*Director*	Now then, Mr Bloggs. Could you tell me something about your background?
	Applicant 2	Well, I used to be a bus driver.
	Director	And?
	Applicant 2	I kept forgetting to stop, so they sacked me.
25	*Director*	(*To himself*) I'm not surprised! (*Aloud*) Okay, let's hear the speech.
	Applicant 2	To be or . . .
	Director	What's wrong?
	Applicant 2	I've forgotten the words.
30	*Director*	To be or not to be.
	Applicant 2	To be or not to be. That is the question. Um . . .
	Director	Oh dear. I'm afraid I can't have someone who keeps forgetting the lines. Who's next?
	Applicant 3	I am!
35	*Director*	Ah, good. Now before your speech, could you just tell me what acting experience you've had?
	Applicant 3	I've never acted before, actually (*sneezes*)
	Director	Well, never mind. What have you done?
	Applicant 3	I used to be a decorator. Now I'm unemployed.
40	*Director*	I see. Okay, would you like to begin?
	Applicant 3	To be or not to be. That (*sneezes*) is the question. Whether (*sneezes and cannot continue*)
	Director	Are you all right?
	Applicant 3	I've got a bad cold.
45	*Director*	Oh no! I must find a Hamlet by tomorrow! What am I going to do?

Stage 3

1 The scene is set in a factory.
What does the factory produce?　　Motor cars
　　　　　　　　　　　　　　　　Chocolates
　　　　　　　　　　　　　　　　Clothes

It is Monday morning and several people are already at work.
What are they doing?　　Working on an assembly line
　　　　　　　　　　　Operating machines
　　　　　　　　　　　Using sewing machines

The supervisor arrives and introduces a new employee. Some-
one has to show the new person what to do.
The new person tells her new colleagues about her previous
job. She says that her previous job was better than this one.
What was her previous job and how was it better?
　　　　　　　　　　　　　　More interesting
　　　　　　　　　　　　　　More pay
　　　　　　　　　　　　　　Better working conditions
　　　　　　　　　　　　　　Nicer workmates

How do the other people respond?
　　Defend their factory and their jobs
　　Agree their jobs aren't very interesting
　　Decide they dislike the new person

How does the scene develop?
　　All the employees decide to leave.
　　They complain to the supervisor.
　　They refuse to work with the new person.
　　They demand a pay rise.

How does the scene end?

2 The scene consists of a TV chat show involving an interviewer and several interesting personalities.

Who are the personalities and what makes them interesting?

An explorer	An eccentric
A pop star	An inventor
A politician	A philosopher

How does the interviewer introduce the programme?
    Describes the personalities himself/herself
    Asks them to introduce themselves
    Asks them questions about themselves

What kind of interaction takes place between the personalities?
    They find they have something in common.
    An argument breaks out.
    They all find something extremely funny.
    They take a dislike to each other.
    They all get annoyed with the interviewer.

How does the programme end?
        They all arrange to go out for a meal.
        There is a fight.
        The interviewer decides to stop the programme.
        They decide to start again.

3 The Social Services/The Army/A Business Company have been having difficulty recruiting people and have decided to mount a national recruitment campaign. As part of the campaign they have decided to produce a television advertisement. Your task is to produce the advertisement.

- What aspects of the work and conditions will you show to attract applicants? What about special perks?
- What sort of applicants do you want to attract? Those with previous experience? Intelligent people? Smart people?

Make sure the advertisement has an introduction, and a clear end.

UNIT 7

Could I see the menu?

Introduction

1 Food *This vocabulary will be of use in the first exercise in Stage 1 and when ordering food in the sketches.*

There are several mistakes in the following lists. Rearrange them so that they are correct.

Starters	Main course	Vegetables	Dessert
Onion soup	Mushroom pizza	Peas	Ice cream
Carrots	Spaghetti bolognaise	Fruit salad	Fresh strawberries
Prawn cocktail	Trout	Sweet corn	Banana split
Melon	Apple pie and cream	Beans	Ham omelette
Pate and toast	Chicken casserole	Cauliflower	Stuffed tomatoes and rice
Avocado	Chilled grapefruit	Steak	Chocolate cake
Roast beef	Pork cutlets	Cabbage	

2 Ordering food *The following dialogue provides language that may be needed in Stage 1 exercise 3 and later sketches in the unit.*

Here is a dialogue between a customer and a waiter. However, it is in the wrong order. Show the right order by numbering each line. (The first and last have been done for you.)

Customer What exactly is Beef Stroganoff? _____

Waiter Would you like some wine? _____

Customer I see. Is there anything you'd recommend? _____

Waiter Good evening, sir, madam. Are you ready to order? __(1)__

Customer Yes, we'll try ½ litre of the house red. __(10)__

Waiter It's a sort of stew. _____

Customer Yes, we'd like vegetable soup and melon to begin with. _____

Waiter Very good, sir. And to follow? _____

Customer Okay, we'll try that. _____

Waiter Well, the Roast Lamb is supposed to be very good. _____

3 In the restaurant   *Throughout this unit you will need the sort of language used by customers and waiters. This exercise presents some phrases that will be of use.*

Match the sentences in Group A with those in Group B.

Group A	Group B
(a) How would you like the steak?	i) They're a kind of prawn.
(b) Is there anything else you'd like, madam?	ii) Could we have peas and carrots, please?
(c) What exactly are scampi?	iii) The steak and kidney pie is the chef's speciality.
(d) What would you like to go with it?	iv) It's chicken soup.
(e) What does the fish come with?	v) No, thank you. Could we have the bill, please?
(f) What's the soup of the day?	vi) It's served with French fries and peas.
(g) What would you recommend?	vii) Medium, please.

4 Complaining   *Making polite complaints will be needed in Stage 3.*

Complete the following sentences. Each gap represents one word.

(a) Waiter, this table-cloth's absolutely filthy. Would _____ _____ changing it, please?

(b) I'm afraid the soup's cold. Would it _____ _____ to change it?

(c) This is ridiculous. We've been waiting half-an-hour already. I'd _____ _____ _____ the manager, please.

ⓓ There seems to be something wrong with the chicken. Do you think _____ _____ have something else?

ⓔ It's terribly draughty here. Could we _____ move to another table?

ⓕ I don't think the bill is quite right. _____ we only ordered one sherry trifle, not two.

ⓖ This fish is completely tasteless. Is it possible to do something _____ _____?

Stage 1

1 Mime Each student mimes eating a type of food while the rest of the class try to guess what it is. The teacher will suggest the types of food for you to mime. When you are miming, help your fellow-students by showing the exact way in which you would eat the food, the size and consistency (eg hard, juicy or chewy etc).

2 Role-play In pairs. One student is a customer in a restaurant and the other student is a waiter. The customer has a chair and the waiter remains standing. Your teacher will give you further instructions regarding your roles.

3 Matching lines Each student is given a line to memorize by the teacher. Each line has a matching line, for example:

Excuse me, this plate's dirty.
    ⓐ Thank you very much sir.
    ⓑ One moment, I'll fetch another one.
    ⓒ Would you like to see the wine list.

The matching line is ⓑ. You have to find the person whose line matches yours. Afterwards, improvise a short scene that includes both lines.

Stage 2

The scene is a restaurant. There are three waiters: one is the head-waiter who has a very superior attitude; the second is foreign and the third is sleepy and not very interested in the job. They are all busying themselves about the restaurant. There are no customers yet.

A customer enters and is met by the head-waiter.

Head-waiter Good evening sir. Let me take your coat.

Customer A table for one, please.

Head-waiter (*To the sleepy waiter*) Would you show this gentleman to a table.

(*The sleepy waiter looks around for a suitable table and very slowly leads the customer to it. The customer sits alone without a menu, but none of the waiters seem to take any notice.*)

5 **Customer** (*Eventually, to the foreign waiter*) Excuse me, but could I see the menu, please?

Waiter 1 The menu? (*Looks puzzled but goes to look for it. After a while he returns with something.*) Here you are.

Customer But this is the wine list.

10 **Waiter 1** Sorry. You don't want wine? What do you want?

Customer (*Angrily*) The menu!

(*The waiter goes and asks the others, then gets the menu. He gives it to the customer and leaves.*)

(*Silence.*)

Customer (*To foreign waiter*) Excuse me, but would you mind taking my order?

15 **Waiter 1** (*Approaching unenthusiastically.*) All right. What would you like?

Customer I'll start with prawn cocktail, then I'll have steak.

Waiter 1 (*Writing slowly.*) Just a minute. Prawn cocktail. Could you spell that please?

20 **Customer** P R A W N   C O C K T A I L.

Waiter 1 And what else?

Customer Steak, please.

Waiter 1 How would you like it?

Customer Rare, please.

25 **Waiter 1** Sorry, what do you mean?

Customer Rare! Not cooked very much!

(*The waiter writes slowly and then leaves without saying anything more. A long pause. The customer is getting more and more upset.*)

Customer (*To head-waiter*) Could I possibly have a half-bottle of wine while I'm waiting.

Head-waiter I'm terribly sorry, but I understood you didn't
30 want wine (*The customer looks annoyed*) (*To sleepy waiter*) Please get the wine list for this gentleman.

(*The sleepy waiter brings the wine list.*)

Waiter 2 Here you are.

Customer A bottle of house red, please.

35 **Waiter 2** House red? Now where did I put it?

Customer Right. That's enough! I'm fed up with this. I'm going!

1 It's someone's birthday and he/she has invited some friends out for a meal.

What sort of people are they?   Lively and noisy
Serious
Snobbish
Drinkers
Formal

The friends enjoy themselves and order a lot of good food and drink.

What do they order?   Every course
The chef's speciality
The most expensive food
Expensive wine

The person whose birthday it is starts to get worried and realises that he/she won't have enough money.

What does he/she do?   Tries to escape from the restaurant
Offers to wash up
Asks everyone for £1 each
Breaks down and cries

2 A number of people are in a restaurant.

Who are they and what is their relationship with each other?
Married couples
Colleagues
Strangers at separate tables
Friends

They order their food but each course that comes is unacceptable in some way.

What is wrong with it?   Overcooked
                                 Undercooked
                                 It tastes like catfood
                                 There is an insect in it
                                 It smells funny

At first the customers ask for their food to be changed, but the new food is equally bad.

How do the customers react?   Some are sick
                                 Some are angry
                                 Some are rude
                                 Some demand their money back

They call the manager, who appears.

What does he/she do?   Offers them money
                                 Confesses that there is no chef
                                 Is very surprised
                                 Offers to eat all the food him/herself
                                 Invites them to lunch at his/her house

How does the scene end?

3 The following report appeared in the Good Restaurant Guide:

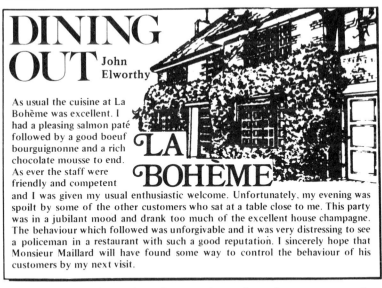

DINING OUT
John Elworthy

LA BOHÈME

As usual the cuisine at La Bohème was excellent. I had a pleasing salmon paté followed by a good boeuf bourguignonne and a rich chocolate mousse to end. As ever the staff were friendly and competent and I was given my usual enthusiastic welcome. Unfortunately, my evening was spoilt by some of the other customers who sat at a table close to me. This party was in a jubilant mood and drank too much of the excellent house champagne. The behaviour which followed was unforgivable and it was very distressing to see a policeman in a restaurant with such a good reputation. I sincerely hope that Monsieur Maillard will have found some way to control the behaviour of his customers by my next visit.

Devise a scene based on the evening when the representative of the Good Restaurant Guide visited La Bohème. How did the restaurant staff treat the representative and what sort of impression did they want to make? What kind of people sat at the table next to the representative and what were they celebrating? What happened when they drank too much? How did the restaurant staff try to cope with the situation? What happened when the policeman arrived and how does the scene end?

UNIT 8

Do-It-Yourself

Introduction

1 Tools and accessories *This vocabulary will be needed in the first exercise of Stage 1, in the sketch for Stage 2 and may be useful in Stage 3.*

Match the pictures with the list of items below.

ⓐ glue	ⓕ a socket	ⓚ a nail	ⓟ pliers
ⓑ scissors	ⓖ a bulb	ⓛ a screw	ⓠ a screwdriver
ⓒ sellotape	ⓗ a fuse	ⓜ a nut	ⓡ a spanner
ⓓ a drawing-pin	ⓘ wire	ⓝ a saw	ⓢ a hammer
ⓔ a plug	ⓙ a ladder	ⓞ a drill	ⓣ a tape measure

48

2 Using the tools and accessories

These expressions and vocabulary will be needed in Stage 1 and may well come in useful later on in the unit.

Choose one of the items in Exercise 1 for each of the following. What would you use to do the following?
  i) make a hole in the wall for a screw
  ii) rewire a plug
  iii) take a nail out of a piece of wood
  iv) undo a screw
  v) tighten a nut
  vi) lay a carpet on the floor
  vii) make a table
  viii) mend a broken radio
  ix) cut some wire
  x) wallpaper a room

3 How to do things

The following instructions will be needed in Stage 1.

The following instructions are not in the right order. Show the right order by numbering them. The first and last one have been done for you in each case. A) are instructions for changing a wheel and B) for putting up a shelf.

A		B	
Let the car down	_____	Screw the supports to the wall	_____
Put on the spare wheel		Saw the wood to the right length	_____
_____		Measure the piece of wood	_____
Jack up the car	_____		
Undo the nuts	_____	Measure the space where the shelf will be	__1__
Take out the spare wheel	__1__	Place the wood on the supports	__8__
Put the jack back into the car	__8__	Paint or varnish the wood	_____
Tighten the nuts	_____	Drill holes in the wall	_____
Take the old wheel off	_____		

Stage 1

1 Mime box

Each student in turn mimes taking an object out of a box and giving it to another student, who should try to use it appropriately. Afterwards the rest of the class say what they thought the object was. Your teacher will tell you which object you should mime.

When it is your turn, try to show what the object is by the way that you hold it. Do you need two hands to hold it or one? Is it heavy? What shape is it?

2 Following instructions You are going to give each other instructions and mime the actions concerned eg saw a piece of wood.

3 Competitive mime In groups. One member of the group goes to the teacher, who whispers to him the first household activity on a list. The students mime to the others what the activity is. As soon as someone guesses correctly, he goes to the teacher, who whispers to him the next activity on the list. The winning group is the one that gets to the end of the list first. Remember that the person miming should not say anything.

Stage 2

The scene is a Do-It-Yourself shop. There are two assistants behind the counter. A customer enters looking rather unsure of himself. He obviously knows nothing about D-I-Y.

Customer Er . . . excuse me, but I wonder if you could help me?
1st Assistant Certainly, sir. What's the problem?
(Customer gets out a plan and unfolds it on the counter.)
Customer This is a plan of my bedroom. I want to build a fitted wardrobe and then decorate the room. I'm afraid I can't afford to get it done professionally.

5

	2nd Assistant	Well, sir, that's the whole point of Do-It-Yourself – you cut down the costs because you do it yourself! Now, let's see what you need.
10		
	1st Assistant	To begin with, you'll need an electric drill. If you'd like to step over here, I'll show you our range.
	(Assistants take customer to look at a range of drills.)	
15	Customer	I've never used one of these before. How do they work?
	1st Assistant	It's quite simple. You turn it on here and press it against the wall like this.
	Customer	I see. Now, what about materials?
20	1st Assistant	Well, for a wardrobe that size you'll need quite a lot of wood. I suggest you use pine.
	Customer	O.K. Now, what about the decorations? I want to put wallpaper on the walls and paint on the ceilings.
	2nd Assistant	(Studies customer's plans and does a few calculations.)
25		I think you'll need 3 gallons of paint and 5 rolls of paper.
	Customer	That sounds okay.
	1st Assistant	Have you got things like brushes, rollers and paste?
30	Customer	No, I haven't anything like that.
	2nd Assistant	Don't forget you'll need some step ladders as well.
	Customer	Oh dear. Do you really think so?
	2nd Assistant	Of course. You must have stepladders *and* you'll need a saw.
35		
	Customer	Oh dear. It seems rather a lot.
	1st Assistant	Not at all. I'll just add it all up.

Stage 3

1 Several people are at a Do-It-Yourself evening class with an instructor.

What is he teaching them to do?
Carpentry
Car maintenance
Picture-framing
Home maintenance
Plumbing

The students have great problems.
In what way?
They are very clumsy.
They are very slow.
The instructor is unclear.
The tools are missing or inadequate.
There aren't enough tools to go round.

Some sort of accident happens.

What is it?   Somebody cuts himself.
Somebody falls off something.
Somebody hurts somebody else.
An argument develops.
There is a fight.

The instructor tries to sort it out.

Then what happens?   They demand their money back.
The instructor walks out.
The students walk out.
The students decide to join another course.
The students appoint another instructor.

2 A couple have recently bought a new house and have invited some guests for dinner. They are anxious to impress their guests.

Who are the guests?   Relations
Superiors from work
Rich friends
Nosey neighbours

During the day the couple have been in a great hurry to complete all the outstanding do-it-yourself jobs in the house.

What have they been doing?   Painting
Mending furniture
Plumbing in the toilet
Rewiring the lights

The guests arrive rather early and not all the jobs have been finished. The couple are worried but the guests make favourable comments. However, as the dinner party progresses lots of embarrassing things go wrong.

What?   The furniture collapses.
The lights fuse.
The toilet floods.
There is wet paint on the chairs.

How do the guests react and how do the couple cope with the situation?

Devise a scene to show the events of the evening. Make sure the scene has a good ending.

3 Make up a sketch to include all the following lines. It does not matter in what order they are used.

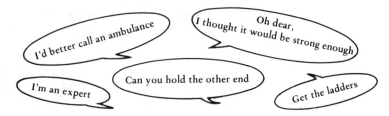

UNIT 9

Can I help you?

Introduction

1 Shopping list *This vocabulary will be needed in the first exercises of Stage 1 and may be useful in Stage 2 and Stage 3.*

Put the following items in the correct list below.

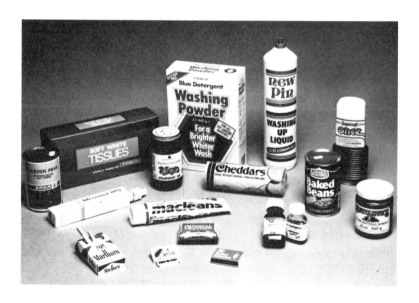

A box of . . . . A packet of . . . . A tube of . . . . A bar of . . . . A jar of . . . . A tin of . . . . A bottle of . . . .

2 Being served *The following dialogue will help you in exercise 2 of Stage 1 and later on in the unit.*

The following dialogue takes place in a small corner-shop between a customer and the shopkeeper. It is in the wrong order. Show the right order by numbering each line. The first and last one have been done for you.

Customer	Seventy-five pence exactly. Here you are.	_____
Shopkeeper	Thank you very much. 'Bye.	_____
Customer	I'd like a tin of tomatoes and two bars of soap, please.	_____
Shopkeeper	'Morning. How can I help you?	_____
Customer	Good morning.	__1__
Shopkeeper	I'm afraid we've sold out of tinned tomatoes.	_____
Customer	Well, in that case I'll have a tin of peas.	_____
Shopkeeper	Right, that's 75p altogether, please.	_____
Customer	'Bye.	__9__

3 Shopping *There are various phrases used in shops that may be of use to you throughout this unit.*

Match the sentences in Group A with those in Group B.

A	B
ⓐ I'm sorry to keep you waiting.	i) I'm afraid we don't.
ⓑ Terrible day, isn't it?	ii) That's all right.
ⓒ I'm afraid they're out of stock.	iii) Yes, if you have a cheque card.
ⓓ You haven't got any onions, have you?	iv) Yes, awful.
ⓔ How much is the calendar over there?	v) I'm sorry, we don't keep spaghetti.
ⓕ Do you take cheques?	vi) Oh, dear. When are you expecting some more?
ⓖ I'd like some spaghetti, please.	vii) That one? I'm afraid it's not for sale.

Stage 1

1 Mime box Each student in turn mimes taking an article out of a box and giving it to another student, who should try to use it appropriately. Afterwards the rest of the class say what they thought the object was. Your teacher will tell you which article you should mime taking out of the box.

When it is your turn, try to show what the object is by the way that you hold it. Do you need two hands to hold it or one? Is it heavy? What shape is it?

2 Role play Pairwork. One student plays the part of a shopper and the other is a shopkeeper. Your teacher will give you further instructions about your role.

3 Matching lines Each student is given a line to memorize by the teacher. Each line has a matching line, for example:

Lovely day, isn't it? ⓐ Over there by the door.
ⓑ Yes, very nice.
ⓒ They're out of stock, I'm afraid.

The matching line is ⓑ. You have to find the person whose line matches yours. Afterwards improvise a short scene that includes both lines.

Stage 2

Scene: A corner shop
It is a cold, wet winter's day. A shop assistant stands behind the counter.
The first customer enters. She is an old, single person who regularly uses the shop.

Shop Assistant	Good morning, Mrs Brown. Terrible weather this morning, isn't it?
1st Customer	It certainly is. I reckon it's the coldest we've had all winter.

(*2nd customer enters, a younger person who has never been to the shop before. He looks worried.*)

5	*Shop Assistant*	'Morning. I'll be with you in a minute.
	2nd Customer	All right.
	Shop Assistant	(*to 1st Customer*) How are you managing in this cold weather?
	1st Customer	Not too bad. A bit lonely, though.
10	*Shop Assistant*	Oh dear! Well, now, how can I help you?

(Mrs Brown searches in her bag for a list. Meanwhile the second customer is looking around and whilst Mrs Brown and the shop assistant are talking, he picks up items from the shelves and slips them into his bag.)

1st Customer I'll have a small box of cornflakes . . . a tin of beans . . . a bottle of milk . . . a small carton of cream.

Shop Assistant Will that be all?

15 **1st Customer** Yes, I think so. How much will that be?

(Shop assistant adds up the amount. Suddenly the first customer notices the second customer slipping a packet into his bag.)

1st Customer Hey, just what do you think you're doing, young man?

Shop Assistant *(looks up)* What's going on?

1st Customer I've just caught him slipping a packet into
20 his bag.

Shop Assistant Let's have a look. Would you mind opening your bag, please?

(The second customer looks shocked and worried, but opens his bag and shakes the contents onto the floor.)

Shop Assistant Good Heavens! . . . two packets of fire lighters, a box of matches, three tins of soup!

25 **1st Customer** And several bars of chocolate.

Shop Assistant Well, what have you got to say for yourself?

Stage 3

1 The scene takes place in a shop. Customers enter one by one. They are all different types.

What sort of people are the customers? Old/young
                Poor/rich
                Shy/confident

There is no sign of the shopkeeper.
What do the customers do? Look embarrassed
           Talk about the weather
           Talk about each other
           Stand in a queue

The shopkeeper still does not appear.
What do the customers think about doing?
Taking what they want without paying
Going to look for the shopkeeper
One of them serving the others
Serving themselves and leaving the money
Leaving the shop and putting 'closed' on the door
Reporting it to the police

They decide on what to do, but something goes wrong.
What?   The shopkeeper returns – there is a fight.
          The shopkeeper turns out to be dead.
          The shopkeeper is locked in the toilet.
          The customers lock the shopkeeper in.
          The police arrive.

How does the scene end?

2   The scene takes place in a supermarket. The customers
have completed their shopping and arrive at the check-out.
What sort of people are they and what have they bought?

All the customers are in a hurry for different reasons.
Why?   One is giving a dinner party tonight.
         One has parked on double yellow lines.
         One is late for a meeting.
         One has to meet a child from school.
         One has a dental appointment.

The person at the front of the queue is holding it up.
Why?   He has no money.
         He cannot understand English.
         He breaks an item of shopping.
         He becomes ill.
         He has an argument with the cashier.

How does the cashier respond?   Sympathetic
                                     Angry
                                     Upset
                                     Calls the manager

What do the customers do?   Get annoyed with the cashier, the manager or the customer
Leave without paying
Try to help the customer with difficulties

How is the situation resolved and how does the scene end?

3 A shopkeeper put this advertisement in the local newspaper.

Many people are impressed by the low prices and come to the shop to buy some goods. Some people travel fairly long distances to take advantage of the bargains. When they arrive they are disappointed and decide that the shopkeeper is cheating them.

Why?   Some of the goods are faulty/poor quality.
He is selling specially made small packages.
The shopkeeper suddenly puts up the prices.
The packages are only half full/empty.

The customers are very annoyed. They argue with the shopkeeper and try to convince him that he has acted unfairly. The shopkeeper is rude and unhelpful.

The customers decide to get their own back on the shopkeeper.
What do they decide to do?   Call a reporter from the local newspaper
Refuse to pay the full price for their shopping
Warn other people not to go into the shop

How does the scene end?

Why don't you try the South of France?

Introduction

1 Leisure activities *This vocabulary will be needed in the first part of Stage 1 and may come in useful in Stage 3.*

Match the pictures with the list below.

(a) fishing
(b) sailing
(c) camping
(d) gardening
(e) darts

(f) billiards
(g) chess
(h) jogging
(i) table-tennis
(j) golf

(k) playing music
(l) tennis
(m) sunbathing
(n) hang-gliding

2 Leisure remarks *This exercise provides more vocabulary that might be of use in Stage 1 and later in the unit.*

In which leisure activity might you hear the following remarks? Choose from the list opposite. Each activity goes with one of the remarks.

(a) It's your turn.
(b) What's on the other channel?
(c) Whose serve is it?
(d) Lie on the floor and put your arms by your sides.
(e) How big's your collection?
(f) Pass me the binoculars.
(g) There's nothing good on this week.
(h) Foul!

i) Playing football
ii) Playing cards
iii) Stamp-collecting
iv) Watching TV
v) Bird-watching
vi) Squash
vii) Going to the cinema
viii) Yoga

3 Making suggestions *In exercise 2 of Stage 1 and later on in the unit you will need to know how to make suggestions. This exercise is to help you with that.*

The following dialogue between two friends is in the wrong order. Show the right order by numbering each line. The first and last have been done for you.

A Well, what are we going to do, then? _____
B Really? I'm not in the mood for dancing. _____
A Good idea! __10__
B What do you suggest, then? _____
A What do you fancy doing tonight? __1__
B I know. Let's go to the pub and think about it. _____
A Oh, no! I'm fed up with going to the cinema. _____
B Well, I'd quite like to go to the cinema. _____
A Actually, I wouldn't mind going to a disco. _____

4 Declining and persuading *As well as declining offers, it will be necessary to know how to persuade in Stage 1 and particularly in Stage 3.*

Match the sentences in Group A with those in Group B.

A	B
(a) Leave me alone, I want to watch this Western.	i) How do you know? You've never tried it.
(b) How about going out for a meal tomorrow night?	ii) I'd like to, but I'm afraid I'm busy tonight.
(c) Aren't you coming swimming this afternoon?	iii) I have to, I'm afraid.
(d) I'm afraid I'm not very keen on camping.	iv) Come on, you can't watch TV all the time.
(e) You must come to Jim's party tonight.	v) I can't afford to go to restaurants.
(f) But surely you're not going to stay in all weekend?	vi) No, I'd rather stay here instead.

Stage 1

1 Mime Each student in turn mimes a leisure activity. As soon as someone guesses what it is, he joins in the activity. For example, if someone is playing cards, you might sit down opposite him and start playing with him.

2 Role play In pairs. It involves two friends who are making plans for the evening. Your teacher will give you further details about your roles.
During the role play continue talking for as long as possible until your teacher tells you to stop.

3 Matching lines Each student is given a line by the teacher to memorize. Each line has a matching line, for example:

Do you want to come with us to the cinema tonight?	(a) The ball's in the corner.
	(b) What are you going to see?
	(c) It's at eight o'clock.

The matching line is (b). You have to find the person whose line matches yours.
Afterwards improvise a short scene that includes both lines.

Stage 2

C is a travel agent.
A and B are a married couple.

    C Good morning.
A+B Good morning.
    C Can I help you?
    A Yes, we're thinking of going on holiday somewhere,
        but we're not sure where.
    C I see. What sort of holiday did you have in mind?

5

A	(at the same time)	Lots of sunbathing.
B		Lots of walking.

C Mm. (*Looks puzzled*) So you'd like somewhere warm?
10 B Not too warm.
A Yes, as sunny as possible.
C And are you interested in the night-life at all?
A Yes. It'd be nice if there were some good discos and clubs we could go to.
15 B Oh, no! Surely that's what we're trying to get away from!
A What do you mean? We never go out at all, so how could we get away from it?
B Well, what's the point of going somewhere where
20 there are lots of people just like here?
C (*interrupting*) Could I just ask what sort of price you want to pay?
B As cheap as possible.
A What do you mean? We want a top hotel.
25 B But we can't afford it.
A Of course we can. We've been saving up all year. (*Their voices rise as they argue. The travel agent looks bemused.*)
C Just a minute, please. (*He pauses.*) I think I can make a suggestion. Why don't you try the South of France? Then one of you can go to the beach and the other can
30 walk in the mountains.
A That sounds like a good idea. And there are some good hotels there.
B No – there are too many English people there!
A Well, then at least we'd have someone to talk to.
35 B But there's no point in going abroad to meet English people! (*C intervenes again.*)
C Excuse me.

Stage 3

1 The scene starts with a person at home on his own.
What is he doing?   Listening to music
Knitting
Reading
Watching TV

What kind of mood is the person in?   Fed up
Tired
Happy
Relaxed

A group of friends arrive.
How do they behave?   They are drunk.
                             They are all bored.
                             They are celebrating.
                             They are excited about something.

The friends try to persuade the person to do something with them.
What do they want to do?   Go to a night club
                             Go to the cinema
                             Go ten pin bowling
                             Go for a meal

How does the person react?   Tries to get rid of them
                             Agrees to go with them
                             Gets annoyed
                             Persuades them to stay

There is an unexpected outcome.
What?   They all stay and the person goes.
       The person has a secret reason for wanting to be alone.
       Someone else arrives.
       The friends argue among themselves.

2   The scene is set in a Sports Centre. A group of people are being taught how to do something.
What?   Yoga
       Gymnastics
       Tennis
       Basketball
       Keep fit

What sort of people are they? Why have they decided to take up this new sport and do they find it easy or difficult to learn? Unfortunately, the instructor is not doing very well.
Why?   She is young and inexperienced.
       Something upsetting has happened to her.
       She is unwell.
       She is bored with her job.

How does the scene develop?   The students are confused.
       Some students are angry and want their money back.
       Someone hurts himself.
       The instructor breaks down and cries.

How does the scene end?   The students agree to help the instructor.
       The instructor leaves (in what sort of mood?)
       A new instructor is sent to the class.
       One of the students takes over the instruction.

3 Read the following letter written to the Customer Relations Director of a large holiday company.

4 Church Street

Middletown

Essex

Monday September 9th

Dear Sir,

I wish to complain about the holiday I recently took with your company at the Hotel Sunrise in Malaga.

This hotel sounded very attractive in the brochure; it had a swimming pool, tennis courts and two bars. It was also described as being situated near the sea.

Imagine our disappointment when my family and I arrived to find that the hotel was only partly built. There was no sign of the swimming pool, tennis courts and two bars, and it was a good ten miles from the sea.

We complained to the receptionist and other hotel staff, but no one was prepared to take us seriously. We demanded to see the manager. After a long argument he agreed that we had grounds to feel annoyed. He made us an offer which, in the circumstances, we accepted in compensation for our disappointment.

I feel we were deceived in booking our holiday at the Hotel Sunrise and I expect your company to repay me at least half the cost of the holiday. Otherwise I shall consider legal action.

Yours faithfully,

G.K.Harris

Your task is to work out a scene based on the arrival of the Harris family at the Hotel Sunrise.

How many people are there in the family? What ages? What sort of characters?
How do the family feel when they first arrive and how does their mood change when they realise what the hotel is really like?
How do the hotel staff deal with their complaints?
What is the attitude of the manager?
What does the manager offer them?
Does the scene end amicably?